MW01286105

ONE HUNDRED
POPULAR PIANO SONGS
for the
WHITE KEYS

Finger Number Songs

To access companion piano music
online, visit
www.smithtylersmusic.com.
Enter code: **PJST-04**

Philippa Smith-Tyler

xulon
PRESS

Copyright © 2015 by Philippa Smith-Tyler

ONE HUNDRED POPULAR PIANO SONGS FOR THE WHITE KEYS
Finger Number Songs
by Philippa Smith-Tyler

Printed in the United States of America

ISBN 9781498421508

www.xulonpress.com

TABLE OF CONTENTS

—ɱ—

INTRODUCTION

This book is intended for fun piano playing for the very young (ages 3 and up) to the very young-at-heart (age 99 and up).

Look at your piano!

The piano or electronic keyboard has white keys and black keys. The black keys are in groups of two and three.

Can you name the piano keys?

In the picture, the name of the white keys from your left to your right are named **F, G, A, B, C, D, E, F**. The white keys below the THREE BLACK keys are named **F G A B**. The white key to your left of the two BLACK keys is always named **"C."**

Naming the keys is *easy-peazy-lemon squeezy*. The keys are named after the first seven letters of the English alphabet.

A B C D E F G

When you get to the letter "**G**," you start all over again with the letter "**A**."

If you have an 88-key keyboard, the lowest white key (the key at the leftmost end of the keyboard) is "**A**."

The highest white key (the key at the rightmost end of the keyboard) is "**C**."

How to play the music in this book.

To play ALL piano music, you must give your fingers the numbers

"**1 2 3 4 5**" on each hand.

The thumb is number "**1**."
The pointer finger is number "**2**."
The middle finger is number "**3**."
The ring finger is number "**4**."
The pinky finger is number "**5**."

The songs listed in this book are called **FINGER MUSIC** because there are only numbers to tell your fingers what keys to play. When you see the letters RH, this means the right hand will play. When you see the letters LH, this means the left hand will play.

Most of the **FINGER MUSIC** songs here are written for the white keys. But there are a few exceptions. Read on. . .

Some songs have interesting symbols.

To be able to play the songs with interesting symbols, you must be familiar with the following:

:‖   is the symbol for **repeat** the previous song or section of a song. [You will see this in **"Rolling In The Deep"** by Adele, song no. 68.]

‖   is the symbol for **the end** of the song. [You will see this in **"Rolling In The Deep"** by Adele, song no. 68.]

is the symbol for the **sharp** which means play the black key directly to the **right** of the white key under your finger [You will find this symbol in **"Sonatina"** by Muzio Clementi, song no. 78 and **"Thriller"** song no. 90.] If your finger number is "4", play the black key to the right instead.

♭   is the symbol for the **flat** which means play the black key directly to the **left** of the white key under your finger. [You will find this symbol in **"Star Wars"** by John Williams, song no. 80.] If your finger number is "3", play the black key to the left instead.

The "Middle C" position

Position your fingers on the piano with both thumbs sharing **"C,"** this is called the **"Middle C"** Position. Remember: The white key to your left of the TWO BLACK keys is always named **"C."**

The RIGHT HAND fingers will play **C D E F G**.

The LEFT HAND fingers will play **C B A G F**.

Put your hands in the **"Middle C"** Position.

NOW! WE'RE READY TO PLAY...

ONE HUNDRED POPULAR PIANO SONGS FOR THE WHITE PIANO KEYS

All songs are arranged for easy playing. Arranger: Philippa Smith-Tyler

An audio file is available to accompany the songs in this text. To obtain this file, access the author's website www.smithtylersmusic.com and enter the code *PJST-04*.

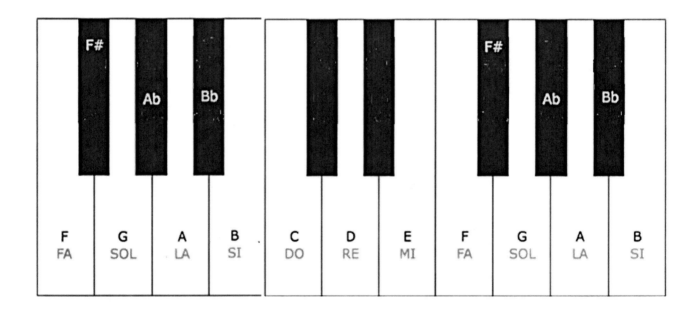

ACKNOWLEDGEMENT

I wish to thank the many piano students from Miami, Florida, to Washington, DC, who have helped create this book by trying out my arrangements and enjoying playing them.

1. A B C

Sung by Michael Jackson

LH   4 3 1
ABC

RH   3   3   2 1–
It's ea - sy as

LH   4   3   1
One Two Three

RH   3 3 2 1–
Like sing-ing

LH   4   3   1
Do Re Mi

RH   2   3   1 --   3   2   1
One Two Three, That's how ea-

LH   3
sy

RH   2 3   1
Love can be!

2. AMAZING GRACE

By John Newton, 1725 - 1807

LH   4 1 –

A-ma-

RH   3 1   3 –   2   1

zing grace, How sweet

LH   3   4 ---

the sound

LH   4   1 –

That saved

RH   3 1   3 –   2 3 5 –

A wretch like me

RH   3 5 3   5 3   1 –

I once was lost

LH   4   3 1 1 3   4

but now I am found

LH   4   1

Was blind,

RH   3 1   3 – 2 1

but now I see.

3. ANTS MARCHING SONG

By John D. Singleton

LH	3	3			

The ants

RH	2	2	3	4	

Go marching one

RH	3	4	2	1	

by one, Hur-rah!

LH	3	1 ---

Hur – rah!

LH	3	3

The ants

RH	2	2	3	4

Go marching one

RH	3	4

by one,

LH	4	3	5	3

Hur-rah! Hur-rah!

LH	5	3	3	3	5

The ants are marching

LH	4	4	4

one by one

LH	4	5	5	5	5	3

The little one stops to

RH	3	3	3

Suck his thumb.

LH	5	4	3	4	5

And they all go march-

RH	3	2

ing down

LH	3	1

to the

RH	2

ground

4. A SAILOR WENT TO SEA, SEA, SEA
Children's Nursery Rhyme

LH   4   1 4   3
A sailor went

RH   3
to

LH   4   4   4
sea, sea, sea

LH   4   1   4   3   3   4   4   4
To see what he could see, see, see

LH   4   1   4   3
And all that he

RH   3
could

LH   4   4   4   4   4
see, see, see was the

LH   4   4   4   4   3   2   1   1   1
bottom of the big blue sea, sea, sea.

5. AIR

("Surprise Symphony"
by Franz Josef Haydn)

RH   1 1   3   3   5   5   3
Papa Haydn's dead and gone

RH   4   4   2   2
But his mem'ry

LH   2   2   4 –
Lingers on

RH   1   1   3   3   5   5   3 – 4   2
When his mood was one of bliss, he wrote

LH   2 4   1
Jolly songs

RH   3   1 –
Like this.

6. ALL NIGHT, ALL DAY

By Clay Evans

LH   **4   1**

All night

RH   **3 2   1**

All – day

LH   **3 1   1   3   1 3 1   1 3 4**

Angels watching over me, my lord

LH   **4   1**

All night

RH   **3 2   1 – 5 3   3   1   2**

All—day, Angels watching o-

LH   **2   1- - -**

ver me.

7. MY COUNTRY, 'TIS OF THEE

By Samuel F. Smith, 1808 - 1895

RH   1   1   2

My country

LH   2   1

'tis of

RH   2   3   3 4 3 2 1 2   1

Thee, Sweet land of liberty, of thee

LH   2 1

I sing.

RH   5   5   5   5   4   3

Land where my fathers died.

RH   4   4   4   4 3   2

Land of the pilgrims' pride

RH   3   4-3-2-1   3   4   5

From every--   mountainside

LH   3-5

Let

RH   3   2   1

Freedom ring!

8. ARKANSAS TRAVELER

LH   4

RH   1   3   2   1

LH   3   3   4   4   1 -----

RH   2   2   3   3   2   3   2   1

LH   3 ---   4 ----

RH   1   3   2   1

LH   3   3   4   4   1 -----

LH   1   2   1   4   3   1   2   3   4   5

RH   3   2   1

9. A-TISKET, A-TASKET

RH **3 5 -- 3 3 5 -- 3**
A tis - ket, a tas - ket,

RH **3 5   5   3 3   5 3**
a green and yellow basket,

RH **3 4   4 2   2 4 4   2 2**
I wrote a let - ter to my love and

RH **5 4   3   2   3 --1**
On the way I dropped it.

RH **3 5 -- 3 3 5 -- 3**
I dropped it, I dropped it,

RH **3   5 5   3 3   5 -- 3**
And on my way I dropped it.

RH **3 4 4   2 --   4   4 2 2**
A lit - tle boy   picked it up and

RH **5 4 3 2   3 --1**
Put it in his pocket.

10. AWAY IN A MANGER

By James R. Murray, 1887

RH   5 5 – 4 3   3 – 2
Away in a manger

LH   1   1   2   3   4 –
no crib for a bed

LH   4   4 – 3   4   4
The little lord Je-

RH   2
sus

LH   2   3   4   1
lay down his sweet

RH   3 – 5 5   4   3
head. I love the lord

RH   3 2
Jesus

LH   1   1   2   3
look down from the

LH   4   4
sky And

RH   4   3   2   3 2
stay by my cradle

RH   1   2
'til morn-

LH   3   2   1 –
ing is nigh.

11. BAA BAA BLACK SHEEP
English Nursery Rhyme

LH	4	4	
	Baa, Baa		

RH	2	2	3
	black sheep, Have		

RH	3 3 3	2	
	you any wool?		

LH   1   1   2   2   3
Yes Sir, Yes Sir three

LH   3   4
bags full.

RH   2   2 2   1 1
One for my master

LH   2   2 2   3
One for my dame

RH   2   2 2   1 1   1
One for the little boy

RH   1
who

LH   2   2   2   3
lives down the lane

LH   4   4
Baa, Baa

RH   2   2   3
black sheep, Have

RH   3   3 3   2
you any wool?

LH   1   1   2   2   3
Yes Sir, Yes Sir three

LH   3   4
bags full.

12. BEAT IT!

Sung by Michael Jackson

RH   3   2   3   2   3   2 3 5   3 2   3

They told him don't you ever come around here

RH   3   2 3 2 3   2   1   2 1 2 1

don't wanna see your face, you better disap-

LH   3   3   1   2 3   3   3   3   2   3

pear. The fire's in their eyes and their words are

LH   4 4 4   3 1 3 3 2 4

really clear. So Beat It, Just Beat It

RH   3 3 1 1 3 3

Beat it, beat it, beat it

LH   2 2

Beat it!

RH   3 3 3   3 5 3 3 3

No one wants to be defeated

RH   2 1 2 1 2 _ 2 1 2 1

Showing how funky strong is your fight

RH   2 1 2 1 2 _ 2 1 2 1 2

It doesn't matter, who's wrong or right, just

LH   1 3 1 3 1 3

Beat it, beat it, beat it!

13. BE KIND TO YOUR WEB-FOOTED FRIENDS

RH   5   5   4   3   3   2 3   3

Be kind to your web-footed friends

RH   2 3   3   2   3   5   3 5   4   2

For a duck can be somebody's moth- er

RH   2   2   1   2   2   1   2   4 ---

She lives in the woods, in the swamp

RH   3   2   3   5 5

Where the weather is

LH   3 3   3 3

very, very

RH   2

dumb!

RH   5   5   5   4   3   3 2 3   3

Now you may think that this is the end.

RH   1   1 1

Well, it is!

14. BE OUR GUEST

from "Beauty and the Beast" by Disney Productions

RH 3 5 1   3 5
Be our guest! Be our

LH 2
guest!

RH 3 5
Put our

LH 3 4
service

RH 3 1
to the

LH 4
test!

RH 3 5
Tie your

LH 3 4
napkin

RH   3   5
'round your

LH 3   4
neck, che-

RH 3 5
rie And

LH 3 4
we pro –

RH 4 2
vide the

LH 4___
Rest.

LH 5 3
Soup du

RH 2
Jour

LH 5   3
Hot hors

RH   1
d'oeuvres

LH   5 3 2 3 2 1 2 _
Why, we only live to serve.

RH 4 5
Try the

LH 3 4   3 4 3 4
grey stuff. It's delicious

LH 3   4 3 4 3 2
Don't believe me? Ask the

LH   3 4
Dishes.

RH   3   5   1   3   5
They can dance. They can

LH   2
sing!

RH   3   5
Af-ter

LH   3   4
All, Miss

RH   3   1
this is

LH   4
France!

RH   5   3   1 1   1   1   1 2
And a dinner here is never

RH   3   1   2
second best

LH   3   3   3
Go on, un –

RH   3 – 3 3 -- 2   1
fold your men- u. Take

LH   2
a

RH   2 ---- 2 2-- 1
glance and then you'll

LH   3   1
Be our

RH   3
Guest

LH   3   1
Be our

RH   3   3   3   1
guest! Be our guest!

15. "BEVERLY HILLS COP" THEME

LH   3   1   3 3

RH   2   1

LH   4   3

RH   3 ---

LH   3 3

RH   4   3   1 –

LH   3 ------

RH   3

LH   3   3   4

RH   3

LH   2   3

16. BINGO
English Children's Folk Song

LH　　4　　1　1　1　4　　3　3　4　　4
There was a farmer had a dog and

RH　　1 1　　2　　2　　3 –　　　1 --
Bingo was his name – o

RH　　3 3　4　　4　　4 --
B – I – N – G – O

RH　　2 2　3　　3　　3
B – I – N – G - O

RH　　1 1　2　　2　　2
B – I – N – G - O

LH　　1　2　　4　3　　2　1 –　　　1 --
And Bingo was his name – o.

17. BLOW THE MAN DOWN

LH   4   4 3   4
Come all ye young

RH   3 1   3
fellows that

LH   4 3 4
follows the

RH   3 –
sea

LH   4 ------ 3 ------
Way --- hey ----

RH   4 3   4   2--
Blow the man down

RH   4   4   5
Now please pay

RH   4 2
atten-

LH   2
tion

RH   2 4 5 4 2 --
and listen to me

RH   5   5   5   5
Give me some time

RH   4   3   2   3
to blow the man

RH   1
down.

18. BROTHER JOHN

RH   1   2   3   1   1   2   3   1

Are you sleeping, Are you sleeping,
Fre - re Jacques, Fre - re Jacques,

RH   3   4   5 --- 3   4   5 ----

Brother John, Brother John
Dor-mez vous, Dor-mez vous?

LH   4 3   4   5

Morning bells are
Son –ne les ma-

RH   3 – 1----

ringing,
tines,

LH   4 3   4   5

Morning bells are
Son –ne les ma-

RH   3 – 1----

ringing,
tines,

LH   1---- 4 -- 1----   1---- 4 -- 1----

Ding, ding, dong, Ding, ding, dong,
Din, din, don. Din, din, don.

19. CINDERELLA, The Work Song
from The Walt Disney Studios

RH   1   2 3 3   3   3 3 1
Cinderella, Cinderella

LH   1 1 1   3   1   3 3 4
All I hear is Cinderella

LH   4   3   4   4
Fix the breakfast

LH   4   3   4   4
Wash the dish-es

LH   3   4   4   4   3   4   4   4 4
Do the mopping and the sweeping. Go

RH   5 5 5 5 5 4 3 2
Up into the attic and go

RH   4   4 4 4   4 3   2 1 3 2
Down into the cellar, Cinderella

LH   1 2
Cinder-

RH   2 1
ella!

LH   2 3 1 1
Cinderella!

20. CLEMENTINE

By Percy Montrose (1884)

LH   1 1 1 4

Oh, my darling

RH   3   3   3 1   1   3   5 5

Oh, my darling. Oh, my darling

RH   4   3   2

Clementine

RH   2   3   4   4   3   2 3   1

Now you're lost and gone forever

RH   1   3   2

Dreadful sor-

LH   4   2

ry, Clem-

RH   2 1

entine.

21. COMIN' ROUND THE MOUNTAIN

LH   4   3 1 1   1   1   3   4
She'll be coming 'round the mountain

RH   3   5   1
When she comes

RH   1   2   3   3   3   3   5   3   2   1   2
She'll be coming 'round the mountain when she comes

RH   5   4   3 3   3   3   2   1
She'll be coming 'round the mountain

LH   1   1   3 3   3   3
She'll be coming 'round the

RH   2   1
Mountain

LH   2   3   4 4   4   4
She'll be coming 'round the

RH   3   2
Mountain

LH   3   2   1
When she comes.

22. DECK THE HALL

RH 5 – 4 3 2 Deck the halls with	**RH** 2 – 3 4 2 3 – Don we now our gay
RH 1 2 3 1 boughs of holly	**RH** 4 5 2 apparel
RH 2 3 4 2 3 – 2 1 Fa la la la la -- la la	**RH** 3 4 5 Fa la la
LH 2 1 – la la	**LH** 3 2 1 -- 2 3 4 – Fa la la --la la la
RH 5 – 4 3 2 1 2 'Tis the season to be	**RH** 5 – 4 3 2 While we sing our
RH 3 1 jolly	**RH** 1 2 3 1 yule tide carols
RH 2 3 4 2 3 – 2 1 Fa la la la la -- la la	**LH** 3 3 3 3 4 – Fa la la la la
LH 2 1 – la la	**RH** 4 3 2 1 – La la la la --

23. DOWN BY THE STATION

RH   1   1   2   3   3   2 1   2 3   1

Down by the station Early in the morn-

LH   4

ing

RH   3   3   3 4   5   5   5   4 4 5 3

Goes the little choo choo trains all in a row.

RH   1   1   1   2   3   3   2   3   1

See the station master pull the han-

LH   4

dle

RH   1   1   3   3   2   3 1

Chug, chug, woo, woo. Off they go!

24. DOWN IN THE VALLEY

LH   **4**
Down

RH   **1 2 3 ---- 1 ---- 3 3 2 1 2 -------**
In the val - ley,   the valley so low._____

LH   **4   2**
Hang your

RH   **2   5 --- 5 --- 4   3   2   1 ------**
Head o - ver. Hear the wind blow.____

LH   **4**
Hear

RH   **1   2   3 -- 1 --- 3 2 1   2 --------**
the wind blow, dear. Hear the wind blow.___

LH   **4   2**
Hang your

RH   **2 5 --- 5 --- 4 3 2 1 ------**
Head o - ver. Hear the wind blow.____

25. DYNAMITE as sung by Taio Cruz

RH 3 3   3   3   2   **RH** 3 3 3   3 2 1
I throw my hands up   I wanna celebrate

RH 1 2 3   **RH** 2 3
in the air   and live

LH 4   3   **LH** 4 3
sometimes,   my life,

RH 1 2   **RH** 1 2
Saying   Saying

LH 1 3   **LH** 1 3
AYO!   AYO!

RH 1 2   **RH** 1 2
gotta   baby,

LH 1 3   **LH** 1   3
let go!   let's go!

26. GLORY, GLORY, HALLELUJAH!

African American Spiritual

RH   5 4   3 5   1 2 3 1

Glory, Glory Hallelujah!

LH   3 2   1 2   1 3 4 1

Glory, Glory Hallelujah!

RH   5 4   3 5   1 2 3 1

Glory, Glory Hallelujah!

RH   1 2   2   1

His truth is march-

L.H.   2   1 –

ing on!

27. GO, TELL AUNT RHODY

By Jean-Jacques Rousseau, 1712-1778

RH   **3**   **3**   **2**   **1**   **1**

Go, tell Aunt Rhody

RH   **2**   **2**   **4**   **3 1**

Go, tell Aunt Rhody

RH   **5**   **5**   **4**   **3 3**

Go, tell Aunt Rhody

RH   **1**   **2**   **1**   **2**   **3**   **1**

The old gray goose is dead.

28. GO, TELL IT ON THE MOUNTAIN
By John Wesley Work (1865)

RH   **3**   **3 2 1**

Go, tell it on

LH   **3 4**   **1**

The moun - tain

RH   **2 2 1** **2** **1** **3 5** **5**

Over the hills and everywhere

RH   **3**   **3 2 1**

Go, tell it on

LH   **3 4**   **1**

The moun – tain

RH   **4 3 3 2 2**   **1**

That Jesus Christ is born.

29. GOOD MORNING

LH   4   4 2

Good morning

RH   2   5 --

to you!

LH   4   4 2

Good morning

RH   2   5 --   2

to you! We're

RH   2

all

LH   1   3   2 4

in our places

RH   2   2

with bright

LH   1   3   2   4

shi-ny faces

LH   4   4   2

And this is

RH 2   5 – 3   2

the way to start

RH 1

a

LH   3   4

new day!

30. HAPPY BIRTHDAY TO YOU!
By Mildred J. and Patty Smith Hill

LH   4 4   3   4   1   2

Happy Birthday To You!

LH   4 4   3   4

Happy Birthday

RH   2   1

To You!

LH   4 4

Happy

RH   5   3   1

Birthday, Dear

LH   2 3

(Name)

RH   4 4   3   1   2   1

Happy Birthday To You!

31. HEAD, SHOULDERS, KNEES AND TOES

RH   1__ 2   1
Head, shoulders,

LH   2   1   3_____
knees and toes.

RH   1__ 2   1
Head, shoulders,

LH   2   1   4_____
knees and toes.

LH   5   3   1
Eyes and ears

RH   4   5   4   3   4   2
And lips and teeth and nose.

RH   3   3 1   2   3   4
Head, shoulders, knees and toes.

LH   5   5   5
Knees and toes.

32. HEIGH HO

LH   4 1 –   2   3 –
Heigh ho, Heigh ho

RH   1   2 3   2   1
it's off to work we

LH   2 – 4 3 1 4 4 3 1 4
Go. *(whistle)*

RH   4   3 – 1   2
Heigh ho, heigh ho

LH   4   3   2   1 –   2   3
Heigh ho, heigh ho, heigh ho

RH   1   2 3   2   1
It's off to work we

LH   2 – 4 3 1 4 4 3 2 1
Go. *(Whistle)*

RH   4   3 –   2   1 –
Heigh ho, heigh ho!

33. HICKORY DICKORY DOCK

LH   2 1
Hicko-

RH   2
ry,

LH   1 2 3   2 –   2   2
dickory dock. The mouse

RH   2   1
ran up

LH   3   2
the clock.

LH   2   2   2
The clock struck

RH   2   2   1   1 3   2   32
One and down he run. Hickory,

LH   1   2 3   4 --
dickory dock!

34. HOME ON THE RANGE

LH	4 4 1	**RH**	2 1
	Oh, give me		all day.
RH	2 3 – 1	**RH**	5-- 4 3 2 3
	a home Where		Home, home on the range
LH	2 3	**LH**	4 4 1 1
	the Buf-		where the deer and
RH	4 4 4 – 4 4	**LH**	1 1 2 1
	falo roam And the		the antelope
RH	5 1 1	**RH**	2 --
	deer and the		Play
LH	1 2 1	**LH**	4 4 1
	antelope		Where seldom
RH	2	**RH**	2 3 – 1
	play.		is heard a
LH	4 4 1	**LH**	2 3
	Where seldom		discour-
RH	2 3 – 1	**RH**	4 4 4 – 4 4 3
	is heard a		aging word And the skies
LH	2 3	**RH**	2 1
	discou-		are not
RH	4 4 4 4 4	**LH**	2 1
	raging word and the		cloudy
RH	3 2 1	**RH**	2 1 --
	skies are not		all day!
LH	2 1		
	cloudy		

35. HUSH LITTLE BABY
By Gladys Rich

LH   4

Hush,

RH   3 3 3 4 3 2 2 2

Little baby, don't say a word

LH 4

Pa

RH   2 2 2 2 2 3

pa's gonna buy you

RH   2 1 1   :‖

a mocking bird.

Verse 2. If that mocking bird don't sing,
Papa's gonna buy you a diamond ring.

Verse 3. If that diamond ring don't shine,
Papa's gonna love you all the time.

36. I BELIEVE I CAN FLY

LH 4 4 1   1
I used to think

RH 2 2 3   3 1 2
That I could not go on

LH 4 4 1   1 2
And life was nothing

RH 2 3   3 1   2
but an awful song.

LH 4 4 1 1
But now I know

RH   2   2 3   3   1   2
The meaning of true love

LH   4   4 1 1
I'm leaning on

RH   2 2 3   3 1 2
The everlasting arm.

LH 1 1 2 3 1
If I can see it,

RH   1   2 3 4 3
Then I can do it

LH 1 1 2   3 4 1
If I just believe it

RH   1   2 3 4 2
There's nothing to it.

RH 3 3 3 2 1 1
I believe I can fly

RH 3 3 3   2 1   2
I believe I can touch

RH 1 1
the sky.

RH 3 3   3 3 3 3 3
I think about it every

RH   3   4 4
night and day

RH 3   3 3   3
Spread my wings and

RH 3 2 2
fly away.

R.H 3 3 3   2 1 1
I believe I can soar

RH   3 3 3 2   2   1
See me running through that

RH 2 1 4
open door.

RH. 3 3 3   2 1 1
I believe I can fly

RH. 3 3 3   2 1 1
I believe I can fly

LH 1 1 1 1 1 1 - 2 - 3
I believe I can fly_____.

37. IF YOU'RE HAPPY

LH   4   4   1 1   1
If you're happy and

RH   1   1   1
you know it,

LH   2   1
clap your

RH   2
hands! *[Clap, clap]*

LH   4   4
If you're

RH   2 2   2 2   2
happy and you know

RH   2   1   2   3
it, clap your hands!
[Clap, clap]

RH   3 3   4 4   4
If you're happy and

RH   4
you

LH   3   3
know it,

RH   4   4   3   3
then your face will

RH   3 2   1   1
surely show it.

RH   3 3   2 2   2
If you're happy and

LH   1   2   2
you know it,

LH   3   2   1
clap your hands!
[Clap, clap]

38. I'VE BEEN WORKING ON THE RAILROAD

LH 1 4 1 4 1
I've been working on

RH 2 3 1
the railroad

RH 4 4 1 2 3
all the livelong day.

LH 1 4 1 4 1
I've been working on

RH 2 3 1
the railroad

RH 3 3 3 2 2
Just to pass the time

RH 3 2
away.

RH 2 2 1 2
When you hear the

RH 3 2
Whistle

LH 1 4
Blowing

RH 4 4 1 1 2 2
Rise up early in the

RH 3
morn

LH 3 2 1 2
When you hear the

LH 1 3 4 1
whistle blowing,

RH 3 4 3 2
Dinah, blow your

RH 1
horn.

39. JACK AND JILL
Tune By James William Elliott (1870)

LH   **1**   **4**   **3** **4**   **1** **4** **3**   **4**

Jack and Jill went up the hill to

RH   **3**   **2** **1**

fetch a pail

LH   **2** **3 4**

of water.

LH   **5**   **5**

Jack fell

RH   **2**

down

LH   **5**

and

RH   **3**   **3**   **1**

broke his crown

LH   **1**   **2** **2**   **3** **2** **1 1**

And Jill came rolling after.

40. JESUS LOVES ME

RH   5 3   3   2   3 5   5
Jesus loves me, this I know

LH   3   3   1 3   3   4   4 - -
For the Bible tells me so.

RH   5 3   3   2   3   5 5
Little ones to Him belong.

LH   3   3   4   1
They are weak and

RH   3 2   1 - -   5   3 5
He is strong. Yes, Jesus

LH   3   1 - -
loves me.

RH   5 –   3 1   3   2 – 5 –   3 5
Yes, Jesus loves me. Yes, Jesus

LH   3   1 – 3   3   4 1
loves me. For the Bible

RH   3   2   1 - -
tells me so.

41. JIMMY CRACK CORN

LH	4 4	1	1	1 2			

Jimmy Crack Corn and I

RH   2   2
don't care.

LH   4   4
Jimmy

RH   2   2   2 1 3   3
Crack Corn and I don't care.

RH   1 1   3   3   3 4
Jimmy Crack Corn and I

LH   3 3 --   3
don't care. My

RH   5 5   4 2 1
master's gone away.

LH   4
I

RH   3
feel

LH   4
I

RH   3
feel

L.H   4
I

RH   3 3 3   4 3   2
Feel in the morning sun.

LH   4
I

RH   2
feel

LH   4
I

RH   2
Feel,

RH   2 5   5   5   4 2   1
I feel in the morning sun.

RH   5
Oh!

LH   4   4   1   1 1 2
Jimmy Crack Corn and I

RH   2   2
don't care.

LH   4   4
Jimmy

RH   2   2   2 1 3   3
Crack Corn and I don't care.

RH   1 1   3   3   3 4
Jimmy Crack Corn and I

LH   3   3 -- 3   4 4
don't care. My master's

RH   4   2 1
gone away.

42. JINGLE BELLS

By William B. Bradbury, 1816 - 1868

RH 3 3 3 – 3 3 3 – 3 5 1 2 3 –
Jingle Bells, Jingle Bells, Jingle all the way.

RH 4 4 4 4
Oh what fun it

RH 4 3 3 3 3
Is to ride in a

RH 3 2 2 3 2 – 5 –
One-horse open sleigh, Hey!

RH 3 3 3 – 3 3 3 – 3 5 1 2 3 –
Jingle Bells, Jingle Bells, Jingle all the way.

RH 4 4 4 4
Oh what fun it

RH 4 3 3 3 3
Is to ride in a

RH 5 5 4 2 1
One-horse open sleigh!

43. JOHN JACOB JINGLEHEIMER SCHMIDT

RH   3   2 1
John Jacob

LH   2
Jin-

RH   4   4   4   4   4   4 4 5   2   3
gle-hei-mer Schmidt! His name is my name, too.

LH   1   3
When ev-

RH   4   4   4   4
er we go out,

LH   3   4
The peo-

RH   3   3   3   3
ple always shout,

RH   3   4
There goes

RH   5   5 5   5 4   3 2   1
John Jacob Jingleheimer Schmidt

RH   5   5   5   5   4   3   2   1
Dah dah dah dah, dah dah dah dah!

44. KUMBAYAH
By James Pierpoint (1857)

RH   1   3 5 5 5

Kumbayah, my Lord

LH   3   3   4

Kumbayah

RH   1   3   5   5   5

Kumbayah, my Lord

RH   4   3 2 ---

Kumbayah

RH   1   3   5   5   5

Kumbayah, my Lord

LH   3   3   4

Kumbayah

RH 4   3   2   2 1

Oh, Lord, Kumbayah!

45. LA CUCARACHA

Mexican Traditional

LH   **4 4   4 1**

La Cucara-

RH   **3**

cha!

LH   **4 4   4 1**

La Cucara-

RH   **3**

cha!

LH   **1 1 2 2   3 3 4**

ya no puede caminar

LH   **4 4   4 2**

Porque no ti-

RH   **2**

Ene

LH   **4 4   4 2**

Porque le fal-

RH   **2 5   5 5 4 3   2   1**

ta! Las dos patitas de atrás.

46. LAND OF THE SILVER BIRCH

RH	**2 3**	**4 2**		

Paddle, paddle,

LH   **3**
oh

RH   **2 3**   **4 2**
paddle, paddle,

LH   **3**
oh

RH   **2 3**   **4 2**
Paddle, paddle,

LH   **3**
oh

RH   **2 1**   **2**
dip, dip, swing!

LH   **3 3 4**   **5**
My paddle's keen

RH   **2**   **2**
and bright

RH   **4**   **4**   **5**
Flashing with

LH   **3**
sil –

RH   **2**
ver!

LH   **3 3 4 5**
Follow the wild

RH   **2**   **2**
goose flight.

RH   **2 2**
Dip, dip

LH   **1**
and

RH   **2**
swing!

RH   **2 2 2**
Land of the

LH   **3 3 3**
silver birch

RH   **2   2 2**
Home of the

LH   **3 3**
Beaver

RH   **2 1 2 1**
Where still the might-

LH   **3 5**
y moose

LH   **4 5 4 3**
Wanders at will

RH   **2   1   2   1**
Blue lake and rock-

LH   **3 5   4 5 4 3   5**
y shore I will return once

RH   **2   2   2 2 2**
More. Boom-diddy-ah

LH   **3**
-da,

RH   **2   2 2 2**
Boom-diddy-ah-

LH   **3**
-da,

RH   **2 1 2**
Boo – oo – oo.

47. LAZY MARY

Adapted from Traditional Italian Song

RH   1 --- 1 1 2   3   5 ---3 1 -----

Laz - y Mary, will you get up?

RH   1   2 ---3 2 --- 3   2 ----

Will you get up, will you

LH   2   4 ----

Get up?

RH   1 --- 1 1 2   3   5 --- 3 1 -----

Laz - y Mary, will you get up?

RH   1 2 ----2

So ear - ly

LH   4 3 2   1 ----- 1 -----

in --- the morn--- ing----?

48. LEAN ON ME

RH   1--- 1   2 3   4 -- 4   3   2   1-----
Some times in our lives, we all have pain

RH   1   2   3   3 -- 2 ---
We all have sor-row,

RH   1- 1 2   3   4 --- 4   3   2   1----- 1   2 3
But if we are wise, we know that there's always to-

LH   2 -- 1 ---
mor-row

RH   3   2   1 -- 3   3   2   1–
Lean on me, when you're not strong.

LH   1 2   3   4 –
I'll be your friend

RH   1   2   3   3 2 - 2 ---
I'll help you carry on

RH   1 -- 3   3   2   1 ----
For, it won't be long

LH   1   2 3   4 –
I'm gonna need

RH   3   2 1   1
Somebody to

LH   2 --- 1–
Lean on.

49. LONDON BRIDGE

RH   2 3   2   1-----
London Bridge is

LH   2   1
Falling

RH   2 ----
Down ___,

LH   3   2 1 ---   2   1
Fall – ing down ____ , fall - ing

RH   2 ----
Down ___,

RH   2 3   2   1-----
London Bridge is

LH   2   1
Falling

RH   2 ----
Down ___,

LH   3
my

RH   2
fair

LH   2   4
La - dy.

50. LONG, LONG AGO
by Thomas H. Bayley

RH   1--- 1   2   3 ---- 3   4 5----

Tell me   the tales   that to me

LH   3   4 ---

were so

RH   3 --- 5----- 4   3   2 ----- 4 ---- 3   2   1 ---

dear, Long, long a - go,   long, long a - go.

RH   1--- 1   2   3 ---- 3 4   5 ----

Sing me the songs   I delight-

LH   3   4 ---

ed to

RH   3 --- 5 ---- 4   3   2 ---- 3   2   1 ----

hear, Long, long a - go,   long a - go.

51. LOOBY LOO

RH	1 1 1 3 1 5
	Here we go looby loo.
RH	1 1 1 3 1 2
	Here we go looby lie.
RH	1 1 1 3 1 5
	Here we go looby loo.
RH	5 5 5 4 3 2
	All on a Saturday
RH	1
	night.
LH	4
	We
RH	1 1 1 1 1
	put our right foot in.
RH	2 3 3 3
	We put our right
RH	3 3
	foot out.
RH	4 5 5 5
	We give our foot

RH	5 5 3
	a shake, shake,
RH	1
	shake.
RH	2 3 --3 2
	And turn ourselves
RH	2 1 – 5
	about. Oh!
RH	1 1 1 3 1 5
	Here we go looby loo.
RH	1 1 1 3 1 2
	Here we go looby lie.
RH	1 1 1 3 1 5
	Here we go looby loo.
RH	5 5 5 4 3 2
	All on a Saturday
RH	1
	night.

52. LOVE SOMEBODY

RH   **1**   **3**   **5 5**   **2 3 4**

Love somebody, yes I do

RH   **1**   **3**   **5 5**   **4 3 2**

Love somebody, yes I do

RH   **1**   **3**   **5 5**   **2 3 4**

Love somebody, yes I do

RH   **3 3**   **2 2 1**   **1**   **1**

I won't tell, I won't tell who.

53. MACARENA

LH   1 – 1 1   1- 1 1 1   1   1
Dale a tu cuerpo a- le- gri- a

LH   1   1   3   4   4   4
Ma- ca- re-na. Que tu

LH   1 1   1 11 11 1   1   1
cuerpo espadacle a- le- gri- a

LH   1   1   3   4
co sa bue- na.

RH   1 – 1 1   1 1 1 1   1   1 1   1   3 5
Dale a tu cuerpo a- le- gri- a Ma- ca- re-na

RH   5 ---- 4   5   3   1
Eh – Ma- ca- re- na!

54. MARY HAD A LITTLE LAMB

By Sarah Josepha Hale (1830)

RH   3 2   1   2 3 3   3 –

Mary had a little lamb

RH   2 2   2 – 3 5   5 –

Little lamb, Little lamb

RH   3 2   1   2 3 3   3 –

Mary had a little lamb,

RH   3   2   2   3 2   1------

Its fleece was white as snow.

55. MARIANNE

Calypso style as sung by Harry Belafonte

RH   3   5   1   3   3   2   4---
All day, all night, Marianne

RH   2   4   4
Down by the

LH   2
Sea-

RH   2   2   1   1------
Side, sifting sand

RH   3 3   5 5   1 3   3   3   2   4---
Even little children love Marianne

RH   2   4
All night

LH   2
All

RH   2   2   1   1------
Day, Marianne.

56. MINUET IN G MAJOR
by J.S. Bach

RH 5 -- 1 2 3 4 5 1 1

LH 3 -- 5 4 3 2 1 1 1

RH 4 -- 5 4 3 2

RH 3 -- 4 3 2 1

LH 2----

RH 1 2 3 1 3 – 2 --

RH 5 -- 1 2 3 4 5 1 1

LH 3 -- 5 4 3 2 1 1 1

RH 4 -- 5 4 3 2

RH 3 -- 4 3 2 1 2-----

RH 3 2 1

LH 2

RH 1 ----

57. MY BONNIE LIES OVER THE OCEAN

LH 4	**RH** 2 1
My	back my
RH 3 2 1 21	**LH** 2 3 2 1
bonnie lies over	bonnie to me.
LH 3 4 1	**LH** 4 1 3
the ocean	Bring back, bring
LH 4	**RH** 2 1
My	Back, Oh,
RH 3 2 1 1	**LH** 2 2 2
bonnie lies o –	bring back my
LH 2 1	**LH** 2 3 2 1
ver the	bonnie to me.
RH 2	**RH** 2 3
sea	To me!
LH 4	**LH** 4 1 3
My	Bring back, bring
RH 3 2 1 21	**RH** 2 1
bonnie lies over	Back, Oh,
LH 3 4 1	**LH** 2 2 2
the ocean	bring back my
LH 4 3	**LH** 2 3 2 1
Oh, bring	bonnie to me.

58. MY DREYDL

RH   5 1   1 2 2   3   1 3   5   5   4   3   2 --
I have a little Dreydl, I made it out of clay.

RH   2   2   2   3   3   4   2
And when it's dry and ready

RH   2   5   4 3   2   1
Then Dreydl I will play

RH   3   5   3   5   3   5   3
Oh, Dreydl, dreydl, dreydl

RH   3 5   5   4   3   2 --
I made it out of clay.

RH   2   4   2   4   2   4 2
And when it's dry and ready

RH   2   5   4 3 2   1
Now Dreydl I will play.

59. COME, ALL YE FAITHFUL

LH 1 1 O come	**LH** 2 – 3 4 An - gels
LH 4 All	**RH** 1 1 O come
RH 1 2 – Ye faith-	**LH** 2 1 Let us
LH 4 – ful	**RH** 2 1 Adore
RH 3 2 3 Joyful and	**LH** 4 Him
RH 4 3 – 2 triumphant	**RH** 3 3 2 3 O come, let us
LH 1 1 – 2 3 2 O come all ye ci-	**RH** 4 3 2 3 4 adore Him. O come
RH 1 2 3 tizens of	**RH** 3 2 1 Let us a-
LH 2 3 4 4 – Beth- lehem	**LH** 2 dore
RH 5 – 4 3 4 – Come and behold	**RH** 1 4 3 – 2 -- Him, Christ
RH 3 – 2 3 1 him born the King	**RH** 1 1 the Lord.
RH 2 of	

60. ODE TO JOY
From Ludwig von Beethoven's *Ninth Symphony*

RH　3 3 4 5

RH　5 4 3 2

RH　1 1 2 3 3 __ 2 2

RH　3 3 4 5

RH　5 4 3 2

RH　1 1 2 3 2 ___ 1 1

RH　2 2 3 1

RH　2 3 4 3 1

RH　2 3 4 3 2 1 2 5 ----

RH　4 ----

RH　3 3 4 5

RH　5 4 3 2

RH　1 1 2 3 2 ___ 1 1

61. OLD MACDONALD

LH   1   1   1   4   3   3   4
Old MacDonald had a farm

RH   3   3   2   2 1 –
EE I, EE I O

LH   4   1   1   1   4   3   3   4
And on that farm he had some ducks

RH   3 3   2 2 1 –
EE I, EE I O

LH   4 4   1   1   1 –
With a quack, quack here

RH   1   1   1 –
Quack, quack there

LH   1   1   1   1   1   1
Here a quack, there a quack

RH   1 1   1   1   1   1 –
Everywhere A quack, quack,

LH   1   1   1   4   3   3   4
Old MacDonald had a farm

RH   3 3   2 2 1 –
E I   E I O!

62. ON TOP OF SPAGHETTI

RH 1 1 3 5 1
On top of spaghet-

LH 3 3 5 4 3 4
ti - all covered with cheese

RH 1 1 3 5 5 2
I lost my poor meat - ball

RH 3 4 3 2 1 ---
when somebody sneezed.

RH 1 1 3 5 1
It rolled off the ta-

LH 3 3 5 4 3 4
ble, right on to the floor.

RH 1 1 3 5 5 2
And then my poor meat - ball

RH 3 4 3 2 1
Rolled straight out the door.

RH 1 1 3 5 1
It rolled in the gar-

LH 3 3 5 4 3 4
den, right under a bush

RH 1 1 3 5 5 2
And now my poor meat - ball

RH 3 4 3 2 1
Is nothing but mush!

RH 1 1 3 5 1
So when you are eat-

LH 3 3 5 4 3 4
ing spaghetti with cheese

RH 1 1 3 5 5 2
Protect your poor meat - ball

RH 3 4 3 2 1 ---
from somebody's sneeze.

63. OVER THE RIVER AND THROUGH THE WOODS
by Lydia Maria Childs

R.H.   5 5 5 5 3 4 5   5   5

Over the river and through the woods

L.H.   4 1   1 1   2   3 4

to Grandmother's house we go.

R.H.   5   4   4   4   4 4 3 3 3   3

The horse knows the way to carry the sleigh

R.H.   3   3   2   2   2 3   2 --

O'er the white and drifted snow.

R.H.   5 5 5 5 3 4 5   5   5

Over the river and through the woods

L.H.   4   1   1   2   3   4

Oh, how the wind does blow!

L.H.   4 1   1   2   3   4

It stings the toes and bites

R.H.   3   1   2 3 3 4   3   2 1

the nose as over the ground we go.

64. POLLY WOLLY DOODLE

RH	1 2 3 3	Oh, I went down
RH	1 2 3 3 1	South to see my Sal
RH	1 1 3 3 3 3	Singing Polly Wolly
RH	4 4 3 3 2	Doodle all the day.
LH	2	My
RH	2 2	Sal, she
LH	2 2	is a
RH	2 2	spunky
LH	2	gal
RH	2 2 5 5 5 5	Singing Polly Wolly
RH	4 4 2 2 1	Doodle all the day.

RH	1 2 3	Fare thee well.
RH	1 2 3	Fare thee well.
RH	1 2 3 3	Fare thee well, my
RH	4 3 2	fairy – fay
LH	2	My
RH	2 2	Sal, she
LH	2 2	is a
RH	2 2	spunky
LH	2	gal
RH	2 2 5 5 5 5	Singing Polly Wolly
RH	4 4 2 2 1	Doodle all the day.

65. POP GOES THE WEASEL

RH   1 1 2   2
All around the

RH   3 5 3 1
mulberry bush

LH 4   1
The mon-

RH 1 2
key chased

RH 4 3   1
the wea-sel

LH 4   1
The mon-

RH 1 2   2
key thought 'twas

RH 3 5 3 1
all- in fun

LH 3 –
POP!

RH 2 4   3 – 1 –
Goes the weasel!

LH 1 1 3   3
Every night when

LH 2 2 4   4
I get home, the

LH   1   1 3 1
monkey's on the

LH   2 --   4 -----
Ta - ble,

LH   5   5   5 4
That's the way the

LH   3 2 1
story goes,

LH 3 –
POP!

RH 2 4   3 – 1 –
Goes the weasel!

66. RAIN, RAIN GO AWAY

RH   5   3   5 5 3

Rain, rain go away

RH   5   5 3 3   5 5   3

Come again some other day.

RH 5 5   3 3   5   5 3

Little *[child's name]* wants to play!

RH   5   3   5 5 3

Rain, rain go away

RH   5   5 3 3   5 5   3

Come again some other day.

67. RING AROUND THE ROSY

RH   5   5   3   3   5 3

Ring around the rosy,

RH   3 5   5   3   3   5 3

a pocket full of posies.

RH   5 3   5 3

Ashes, ashes

RH   3   5   5   1

We all fall down.

68. ROLLING IN THE DEEP

(For this piece put both thumbs on the F key.)

By Adele

RH   3 --- 3---- 2 1

LH   3

RH   3 3 2 1

LH   3

RH   3 5 --- 3---- 2 1

LH   3 3 1 1 2 3 3 :|| *[Repeat from beginning of song.]*

LH ||: 3

RH   3 – 3 -- 2 1

LH   3 3 3

RH   3 3 2 --- 3 5 3 2 1

LH   3 3 1 1 2 3 3 :|| *[Repeat from ||:]*

RH   3 5 3 5 3

LH   3 ----- 2 -- 4 ----

RH   3 5 3 5 3

LH   3 ----- || **[The end of the song]**

69. ROW, ROW, ROW YOUR BOAT

RH   1   1   1   2   3

Row, row, row your boat

RH   3 2 3 4 5

gently down the stream

LH   1 1 1 4 4 4

Merrily, merrily,

RH   3 3 3   1 1 1

merrily, merrily

RH   5 4 3 2 1

Life is but a dream.

70. SET FIRE TO THE RAIN

by Adele

LH 5 5 4 3 3 3 4 3
But I set fire to the rain

LH   3 3 4 4 4   5 4
Watched it pour as I touched your face,

RH 2 2 4   2 2 4
Well, it burned while I cried,

RH   2 2 4   2 2 2 2
'Cause I heard it screaming out

RH 2   1
your name,

LH 1   3
your name,

LH 3 3 3 3 3 4   3
I set fire to the rain,

LH   3 3 4 4 4 4 5   4
And I threw us into the flame

RH 2 2 4   2 2   4
Well, It felt something died

RH 2 2 4 2 2 4 2 4 2
'Cause I knew that that was the last time,

RH 2 2 1
The last time.

71. SHOO FLY

RH 3 1   2   3 4   2
Shoo fly, don't bother me.

RH   2
Shoo

LH 2
fly,

RH 1   2 3   1
don't bother me.

RH   3 1   2   3 4   2
Shoo fly, don't bother me.

RH 2   5 5 5 4   3   2 1
'Cause I belong to somebody.

LH 4
I

RH 3
feel,

LH 4
I

RH 3
feel,

LH 4
I

RH 3 3 3   4 3 2
Feel in the morning sun.

LH 4
I

RH 2
feel,

LH 4
I

RH 2   25 5 5   4   2   1
feel, I feel in the morning sun.

RH 5
Oh!

RH 3 1   2   3 4   2
Shoo fly, don't bother me.

RH   2
Shoo

LH 2
fly,

RH 1   2 3   1
don't bother me.

RH 3 1   2   3 4   2
Shoo fly, don't bother me.

RH 2   5 5 5 4   3   2 1
'Cause I belong to somebody.

72. SHOUT, SING, CELEBRATE

RH   1   3 3 1
Shout, sing cele-

LH   4   3 1 3 4 1
brate! Jesus is ri-ding

RH   3
by.

LH   3 1
Dance with

RH   4
Joy!

LH   4 1
Clap your

RH   3
hands

RH   3 3 1 1 3 2
Sing praises to the sky!

RH   1   3 3 1
Shout, sing cele-

LH   4 1
brate! Let

RH   4 4 3 1 1
Out a joyous cry

LH   3 3 1
Everyone

RH   4
shout

LH   3 4 1
"Hosannah!"

RH   4 3 1 1
Wa-ving your palm

RH   2
Branch –

LH   2 1
es high!

73. SILENT NIGHT

LH	4 - 3 4	
	Si - lent	
RH	3	
	night,	
LH	4 - 3 4	
	Ho - ly	
RH	3	
	night,	
RH	2 2	
	All is	
LH	2	
	calm,	
RH	1 1	
	all is	
LH	4 3 3	
	bright. Round yon	
LH	1- 2 3	
	Vir - gin	
LH	4 3 4	
	Mother and	

RH   3
Child

LH   3 3 1 2 3
Ho - ly infant so

LH   4 3 4
tender and

RH   3
mild

RH   2 2 4 2
Sleep in heaven -

LH   2 1 -
ly pea-

RH   3
ce –

LH   1 - 4
Sleep---

RH   3 5 4 2 1___
in heavenly peace.

74. SKINAMARINK

RH 5 5 5 5 3
Skinamarink-a-

LH 3 3 3
dink-a-dink

RH 5 5 5 5 3
Skinamarink-a-

LH 3
Doo

LH 4 3 2
I love you.

LH 3 3 3 3 3 2 2 2
Skinamarink-a-dink-a-dink

LH   3 3 3 3 3 2
Skinamarink-a-doo

LH   3 2 4 4
'Deed I do. I

RH 1 1 1 1 1
love you in the morn-

LH 4 4 3 3 3 3 3 3
ing and in the afternoon. I

RH 2 2 2 2
love you in between

LH 3 3 1 1 2 3
times and underneath the

LH 4 4
moon. Oh.

RH 5 5 5 5 3
Skinamarink-a-

LH 3 3 3
dink-a-dink

RH 5 5 5 5 3
Skinamarink-a-

LH 3 4
Doo. I

RH 3 1
Love you.

75. SKIP TO MY LOU

RH   3   1   3   3 3   5

Skip, skip, skip to my lou

RH   2

Skip,

LH   2

skip,

RH   2   2 2   4

skip to my lou.

RH   3   1   3   3 3   5

Skip, skip, skip to my lou

RH   2   3 4   3   2   1 1

Skip to my lou, my darling.

76. SOMEWHERE OVER THE RAINBOW

LH   1   1   2 4   3   2   1
Somewhere over the rainbow

LH   3   3   4
Skies are blue.

RH   4   4   3 1 2   3   4   2
Somewhere over the rainbow, dreams

LH   2   1
really

RH   2   3   1
do come true.

LH   1   1 2 4   3   2   1
Somewhere over the rainbow

LH   3   3   4
Blue birds fly

RH   4   4 3 1   2   3   4   2
Birds fly o- ver the rainbow, why

LH   2 1
Oh then,

RH   2   3   1
Why can't I?

77. SOMOS EL BARCO

by Peter, Paul and Mary

RH	**3 4 5**			

Somos el

LH **3 3**

barco,

RH **4 4**

somos

LH **3 4**

el mar,

RH **3 3 3 2 1 4**

Yo navego en ti,

RH **2 2 2 1 2 3**

tu navegas en mi

RH **3 4 5**

We are the

LH **3**

boat,

RH **4 4**

We are

LH **3 4**

the sea.

RH **3 2 1 4**

I sail in you

RH **2 1**

You sail

LH **2 1**

in me.

78. SONATINA
by Muzio Clementi

RH 1 – 3 1	*RH 2 3 4# 5
LH 4 4	RH 1 – 3 1
RH 1 – 3 1	LH 4 4
LH 4	RH 1 – 3 1
RH 5 – 4 3 2 1	LH 4
LH 2 1 2 1	RH 5 – 4 3 2 1
RH 2 –	LH 2 1 2 1
LH 1 2 3 4 ----	RH 2 –
RH 1 -- 3 1	LH 1 2 3 4 ----
LH 4 4	LH 1 4 1
RH 3 – 5 3 1 –	RH 3 3 -- 3 1 3
RH 3 1 2	RH 5 -- 1 5 4 3 2
LH 2 1 3 2 4 3	RH 1
*LH 5# 4 3 2 1	

* # is the symbol for the **sharp** which means play the black key directly to the **right** of the white key under your finger.

79. SONG OF THE VOLGA BOATMEN

LH   1   3

Yo, ho

RH   2

Heave

LH   3 -- 2

Ho. O

LH   1   3

Yo, ho

RH   2

Heave

LH   3 -- 2

Ho. O

RH   1   4

Pull to-

RH   3   2

ge – ther

LH   1   3

Yo, ho

RH   2

Heave

LH   3 --

Ho.

80. STAR WARS
By John Williams

LH 4 -- 4 4	RH 4 3 2 1 1 2 3 2
RH 1 -- 5 – 4 -- 3 2 1--	LH 3 2__ 4 4 3 3
LH 4 ----	RH 4 3 2 1 5 2___
RH 4 -- 3 2 1—	LH 4 4 3 3
LH 4 ----	RH 4 3 2 1 1 2 3 2
RH 4 3 4 2____	LH 3 2
LH 4 -- 4 4	RH 5 5
RH 1 -- 5 – 4 -- 3 2 1--	*LH 1 2$^\flat$ 3$^\flat$ 4 5 5
LH 4 ----	LH 4 __ 4 -- 4 4
RH 4 -- 3 2 1—	RH 1 -- 5 – 4 -- 3 2 1--
LH 4 ----	LH 4 ----
RH 4 3 4 2_____	RH 4 -- 3 2 1—
LH 4 4 3__ 3	RH 1 1 1 1------

* $^\flat$ is the symbol for the **flat** which means play the black key directly to the **left** of the white key under your finger.

81. SWING LOW, SWEET CHARIOT

African American Spiritual

RH   3   1 –   3   1 ---
Swing low, Sweet char-

LH   1 3 4
ri- ot ---

RH   1   1   1   1   3 3 5   5 ----
Com- ing for to carry me home.

RH   5   3 –   5   1 ---
Swing low – Swing char –

LH   1 3 4
ri – ot –

RH   1   1   1   2   3   3   2 –   1
Com- ing for to car-ry me home.

82. TEN LITTLE INDIANS

By Septimus Winner, 1888

RH   1   1-1   1   1-1   3   5-5   3-2-1
One little, two little, three little Indians,

RH   2   2-2   2   2-2
Four little, five little,

LH   2
six

RH   2-2
little

LH   2-3-4
Indians

RH   1-1   1-1   1   1-1   3   5-5   3-2-1
Seven little, eight little, nine little Indians,

RH   5   4-4   3-3-2   1   1   1
Ten little Indian boys and girls.

83. THE EENCY BEENCY SPIDER

LH   4   1   1
The eency

RH   1 2   3   3   1   2   1   2   3   1
beency spider went up the water spout.

RH   3   3   4   5   5   4   3   4   5   3
Down came the rain and washed the spider out.

RH   1   1   2   3   3   2   1 2   3   1
Out came the sun and dried up all the rain.

LH   4   4   1 1
Then the eency

RH   1   2   3 3   3   2   1   2   3 1
beency spider went up the spout again.

84. THE FARMER IN THE DELL

LH   4   1 1   1 1   1
The farmer in the dell

RH   2   3   3   3 3   3
The farmer in the dell

RH   5 – 5 – 5   5 3 1
Hi, Ho, the dairy oh

RH   2   3   3   2 2   1
The farmer in the dell

85. THE MULBERRY BUSH

English Nursery Rhyme

RH   1   11   1   3 5 53   1

Here we go 'round the mulberry bush,

RH   1   2 22   2 3 22

The mulberry bush, the mulber-

LH   2 4

ry bush.

RH   1   11   1   3 5 53   1

Here we go 'round the mulberry bush

RH   1 22

So early

LH   4 41   1

in the morning.

86. THE ROSE

By Amanda McBroom, 1977

R.H. 1   2   3 ----
Some say love,

R.H. 3 4 3 3 2 ----
It is a river

R.H.   2   1 ----
That drowns

R.H.   1   2   3   3-
the tender reed.

R.H.   1   2   3 ----
Some say love,

R.H. 3 4 3 3 2 ----
It is a razor

R.H.   2   1 ----
That leaves

R.H.   1   2   3   3-
your soul to bleed.

R.H.   3   4   5 -----
Some say love,

R.H. 5 5 5 5
It is a hun-

L.H. 3 ---
ger,

R.H.   3   4 --3 2   1
An endless aching

L.H. 4 ----
need.

R.H. 1 2   3 ----
I say love,

R.H. 3 4 3   3 2 ----
It is a flower,

R.H.   2   1 ----
And you,

R.H. 1 2 1   1----
Its only seed.

87. THE SNAKE DANCE
By Sol Bloom, 1893

LH 3 2 1 ----- 2 ---- 3 ---- 3 2 1

RH 3

LH 2 1 3 -----

LH 3 2 1 ----- 2 ---- 3 ---- 3 2 1

RH 3

LH 2 1 3 -----

RH   1 2 3 3 3 4 3 2

LH   2 1

RH 2 2 2 3 2 1

LH 3 2 1 ----- 2 ---- 3 ---- 3 2 1

RH 3

LH 2 1 3 -----

88. THIS OLD MAN

Traditional

RH   5   3   5 – 5   3   5 --

This old man, he played One.

LH   3

He

RH   5   4   3   2   3   4

played nick nack on my thumb

RH   3 4   5   1   1 1   1

With a nick nack paddy whack

RH   1   2   3 4   5

Give the dog a bone

RH   5   2   2   4   3 2   1

This old man came rolling home.

89. THREE BLIND MICE

By Thomas Ravenscroft, 1609

RH   3   2   1–   3   2   1–
Three blind mice, three blind mice

RH   5   4   4   3–   5   4   4   3
See how they run, see how they run

LH   4   1   1   2 3   2   1   4   4
They all ran after the farmer's wife

LH   4   1   1   1   2   3   2   1 4   4
She cut off their tails with a carving knife

LH   4   4   1 1   2   3   2   1   4   4   4
Did you ever see such a sight in your life

RH   4   3   2   1
As three blind mice.

90. THRILLER

As sung by Michael Jackson

LH   3   3   2 1 ___
It's close to mid –

3____
night

   4   3   3   4
something evil's

   3   4   3   1   3_____
lurking in the dark.

3 3   2
Under the

1 ___ 3____
moonlight

   4   4 3 3   4
you see a sight that

   3   4   3   1   3___
almost stops your heart.

3   1
You start

RH   3   2 ___ 2
to scream but

2   1 1
terror takes

LH   2   2   3   3   2
the sound before you

   1   3_____
make it.

3   1
You start

RH   3   2   ___2   2   1
to freeze___as horror

LH   1   2   2
looks you right

RH   1 2   1
between the

3_____
eyes_____.

RH   1   2 1   3_
You're paralyzed!

RH   3   5 3
'Cause this is

LH   3___   4___
thrill - ler,

RH   5   4#   3
thriller night!

RH   3   3 2   2 1
And no one's gonna

LH   1   3   1
save you from

RH   2   3   3 2   1
the beast about to

           3
Strike

RH   3   5   3
You know it's

LH   3___   4___
thrill - ler,

RH   5 4# 3
thriller night!

RH   3   3 2   2
You're fighting for

           1   1   1 2   1
your life inside a

RH   3 3 __ 5   5 3 -
Kil - ler, thriller to

LH   3___
night!

91. THROUGH THE WOODS
(Welsh Folk Tune)

LH 4 1

RH 3 5 4 3 1

RH 1 2 4 3 2 1

LH 2 4 4 1

RH 3 2 1

LH 2 3 5 3 4 1

LH 2 1 --

92. WE WISH YOU A MERRY CHRISTMAS

16th Century English Carol

LH 4 1
We wish

RH 1 2
you a

LH 1 2 3 3
merry Christmas.

LH 3
We

RH 2 2 3 2 1
wish you a merry

LH 2 4 4
Christmas. We

RH 3 3 4 3 2
wish you a merry

LH 1 3 4 4
Christmas and a

LH 3 --
hap-

RH 2 --
py

LH 2 1 --
New Year.

LH 4 1 1
Good tidings

LH 1 2 -- 2 1 2
to you, To you and

LH 3 4 --
Your king.

RH 2 3 2 2
We wish you a

RH 1 1 5
merry Christ-

LH 4 4 4 3
mas and a hap-

RH 2
py

LH 2 1 --
New Year!

93. WHEN JOHNNY COMES MARCHING HOME
by Louis Lambert

LH   3   3
When John-

RH   2 2   2 --   3 4   3 4   2 1 --
ny comes march - ing home again, Hurrah!

LH   3 1 -- 3 3
Hurrah! We'll give

RH   2 2 2 -- 3 4 3 4 5 --
him a hearty welcome then. Hur-

LH   3 – 5 3 --
rah! Hurrah!

LH   5 3   3 3   4 5 4   4   4
The men will cheer and the boys will shout

RH   4 4   4 2   3 3   3   4 5
Ladies they will all turn out. And we'll

LH   3 4 5
all feel glad

RH   3
When

LH   3
John –

RH   2 2   2 1 2
ny comes marching home.

94. WHEN SHE LOVED ME

by Randy Newman

LH   4   1   1 2 1   4 – 3 1
When somebody loved me, every

RH   1   3   2 1 2 –
thing was beautiful

LH   2
Ev-

RH   2   3 – 2   1   2 3 5
ery hour we spent together,

LH   3   4 3   1
lives within my

RH   2 –
heart

LH   4   1   1   2   1 3   1   1
And when she was sad, I was there

RH   3 2   1   2 –
to dry her tears

LH   2
And

RH   2   3 2   1 2 3 5
when she was happy, so was

LH   3 –
I

RH   4   3 – 2 -- 1 --------------
When she loved me.

95. WHISTLE WHILE YOU WORK

By Frank Churchill, 1937

RH   5   5   4   3   4   5 –

Just whis-tle while you work.

RH   5 5 4 3 4 5 –

(Whistle)

RH   5 5   4   3   2   5   4   3

Put on that grin and start right in

RH   2 5 4   3   2   5 –

to whistle while you work.

RH   5   5   4 3 4   5 - - -

Just hum a merry tune.

RH   5 5 4 3 4 5 –

(Whistle)

RH   5   5   4   3   2   5   4   3

Just do your best, then take a rest

RH   2   5 4   3   2   1 –

And sing your-self a song.

96. WHO'S AFRAID OF THE BIG BAD WOLF

By Frank Churchill, 1937

RH   5   3   1
Who's afraid

LH   4 4   5
of the big

RH   3   2 –
bad wolf

LH   4   5
the big

RH   3   2 – 4   3   2   1
bad wolf, the big bad wolf

RH   5   3   1
Who's afraid

LH   4 4   5
of the big

RH   3   2 –
bad wolf

LH   5
La

RH   3 2
La, la

LH   4 1 –
La lah.

97. YANKEE DOODLE

By Frank Shuckburgh, 1776

RH 1 1 2 3
Yankee Doodle

1 3 2 –
came to town

RH 1 1 2 3 1 –
Riding on a po-

LH 2 – 4
ny! He

RH 1 1 2 3 4
Stuck a feather in

3 2 1
his hat and

LH 2 4 3 2 1–
Called it mac-a-ro-

LH 1
ni!

LH 3 2 3 4
Yankee Doodle,

LH 3 2 1
keep it up!

LH 4 3 4 5
Yankee Doodle

RH 3 --- 5 ---
Dan – dy

LH 3 2 3 4 3
Mind the music and

LH 2 1 3 4
the step and with

RH 2
the

LH 2
girls

RH 2 1 -- 1 ---
Be han- dy. ---

98. YOU ARE MY SUNSHINE
As sung by Jimmie Davis in 1940

LH   4 1
You are

RH   2   3 – 3 –   3   2 3   1-- 1 –
My Sun-shine, my only sun-shine

RH   1   2   3   4 –
You make me hap-

LH   3 -- 3 --
py -- when

RH   5   4   3 --- 1   2 3   4 ---
skies are gray. You'll never know,

LH   3 -- 3 --
Dear, how

RH   5   4   3 --- 1
much I love   you.

RH   1   2   3-- 4 2 2   3 1 --
Please don't take my sunshine away.

99. YOU PUT MY LOVE ON TOP

as sung by Beyonce' Knowles

LH   4   3   1
Ba - by it's

RH   3 --
you.

LH   1   3   1 3 1
You're the one I love.

LH   1   3   1 3 1
You're the one I need.

LH   4   3   1 3
You're the only

RH   2
one

LH   3 4
I see.

LH   4   4 4 3   1
Come on baby it's

RH   3
you.

LH   4   3   1   3   1
You're the one that gives

LH   3   1
your all.

LH   4   3   1 3 4
You're the one I can

RH   2
al-

LH   3   4
ways call.

LH   4 3 1   4   4
When I need you make

LH   4 3 1   1   431
everything stop! Finally

LH   4   3   4   1   3   1
you put my love on top!

100. YOU'VE GOT TO BE CAREFULLY TAUGHT

(From "South Pacific" by Rodgers and Hammerstein)

RH   5   5 3 4   5 – 5 4 – 2 4 –
You've got to be taught to hate and fear

RH   4   5 3 4 5   5   4 – 2 4 –
You've got to be taught from year to year.

RH   4 3 1 2   3 –   4 5   2 –
It's got to be drummed in your dear

LH   2 1
little

RH   2   2
ear. You've

LH   1   3 2 1   3 2   1 --
got to be carefully taught.

101. HEART AND SOUL

LH   1   1   1 ------ 1   2   3   2   1

RH   2   3   3   3 ----

RH   3 2   1 2   3   4   5 ------ 1 --

RH   5   4   3   2   2

LH   1 ---- 2   3 ---- 4   5 --- 4   3   2

LH   1   1 1 ------ 1   2   3   2   1 --

RH   2   3   3   3 ----

RH   3 2 1 2   3   4   5 ------ 1 --

RH   5 4 3 2 2

LH   1

CPSIA information can be obtained at www.ICGtesting.com
Printed in the USA
BVOW04s1333240715

410142BV00013B/20/P